Made Whole Devotional

FOR BREAST CANCER CONQUERORS

20 Devotions For Healing And Comfort

CHARRON WALKER

Made Whole Devotional

Copyright © 2024 by Charron Walker. all rights reserved.

Some information in this book has been previously published in My Purpose God's Plan.

Published by Charron Walker Tampa, FL

No part of this publication may be reproduced, stored in a retrieval system or transmitted in any way by any means, electronic, mechanical, photocopy, recording or otherwise without the prior permission of the author except as provided by USA copyright law.

Book design copyright © 2024 all rights reserved.
Cover and Interior Designs by thecornerstonepublishers.com

Published in the United States of America

ISBN: 978-1-965593-02-8

Scriptures marked MSG are taken from The Message®. Copyright © 2002 by Eugene H. Peterson. Used by permission of NavPress. All rights reserved.

Scriptures marked NKJV are taken from New King James Version®. Copyright © 1982 by Thomas Nelson. Used by permission. All rights reserved.

Scriptures marked AMP are taken from Amplified Bible®. Copyright © 2015 by The Lockman Foundation. Used by permission. All rights reserved.

DEDICATION

To my conquering sisters:

I was diagnosed at the age of 32 and my mom passed away from this disease at the age of 33. I had big plans for myself after graduation. I was going to find a good-paying job in human resources, pay off my student loan, and begin to move into the next stage of my life. I wanted to get married, have children, get a dog, and have a big house with the white picket fence.

In a matter of days, everything changed. I found a lump in my right breast while I was in the shower doing a monthly self-breast exam. I went from the mountaintop to the valley, from joy to depression, and from hope for the future to no hope at all.

I felt like I was in a whirlwind. I was feeling a variety of emotions: fear, denial, hopelessness, and panic, just to name a few. I remember thinking, "I am thirty-two years old, and I just got my master's degree. I have my whole life ahead of me and now I have been given a death sentence. What did I do wrong?"

The purpose of this book is to bring hope to women, young and old, who are diagnosed with and have overcome breast cancer. It's a long journey, with many peaks and valleys, good days and bad days, joyful moments and sad moments, courageous times, and fearful times. But through it all, God is always there by your side, waiting for you to reach out to Him.

Be strong. Take courage. Don't be intimidated. Don't give them a second thought because GOD, *your God, is striding ahead of you. He's right there with you. He won't let you down; He won't leave you.*

DEUTERONOMY 31:6 MSG

CONTENTS

DEDICATION ii

1. Feelings Of Fear 1
2. Feelings Of Anxiety 6
3. Feelings Of Hopelessness 11
4. Feelings Of Depression 16
5. Feelings Of Anger 21
6. Feeling Confused 25
7. Feelings Of Panic 29
8. Feelings Of Denial 35
9. Feeling Overwhelmed 39
10. Feeling Stressed 43
11. Feeling Worried 48
12. Feelings Of Frustration 52
13. Feeling Negative 56
14. Feeling Doubtful 60
15. Feeling Discouraged 64

16. Feelings Of Sadness 68

17. Feelings Of Urgency 73

18. Feelings Of Insecurity 77

19. Feeling Anxious 82

20. Feeling Ashamed 86

21. Tools For Your Toolkit 90

END NOTE 117
ABOUT THE AUTHOR 118
ABOUT YOUNG SURVIVORS NETWORK
OUTREACH MINISTRY, INC 119

But He was wounded for our transgressions,
He was bruised for our iniquities;
The chastisement for our peace was upon Him,
And by His stripes we are healed.

ISAIAH 53:5 NKJV

1
FEELINGS OF FEAR

Even when the way goes through death valley, I'm not afraid when you walk at my side. Your trusty shepherd's crook makes me feel secure.

Psalm 23:4 MSG

Merriam-Webster Dictionary Definition: An unpleasant often strong emotion caused by anticipation or awareness of danger.

Being afraid is a natural response to something that is a new experience. Fear can keep you trapped in a cave of uncertainty because of the unknown. It can cause physical, emotional, and psychological symptoms. Fear will make you imagine all types of negative outcomes, especially when you have previous information or knowledge about a subject or person. My fear meter went from one to one million when I was diagnosed with breast cancer because I knew I had a family history and that my mom passed away from this disease at a young age. Fear took over my thoughts to the point that it affected my sleep. I thought the odds were stacked against me, but God had another plan. He already knew the outcome, but I needed to do my part and trust Him in the dark. It's during these times when you can't see the way before you that I call blind faith. You must keep moving. You must keep fighting. You must keep pushing your way through fear until you see daylight.

> *Don't panic. I'm with you. There's no need to fear for I'm your God. I'll give you strength. I'll help you. I'll hold you steady, keep a firm grip on you.*
> **Isaiah 41:10 MSG**

I knew of God because I grew up in church, so I was familiar with praying and reading my Bible. But it wasn't until that moment that I began to know God on a personal and intimate level. I had to dig deep inside myself. I had to remember God's promises in His word and hold on to them for dear life. My relationship with God made the journey a little easier to bare because I knew He was in control. Turn it all over to God and let His peace surpass your understanding. I pray that this new journey you are on strengthens your faith and trust in God.

> *When I get afraid, I come to you in trust.*
> **Psalm 56:3 MSG**

Prayer: *Father, help me to see past what's in front of me even though it's fearful and I don't know the outcome. Help me to trust you despite what it looks like. Thank you for your strength and your grace to continue my journey. In Jesus' name, amen.*

Are you fearful right now? What can you do to push through that fear?

CHARRON WALKER.

2
FEELINGS OF ANXIETY

I've told you all this so that trusting me, you will be unshakable and assured, deeply at peace. In this godless world you will continue to experience difficulties. But take heart! I've conquered the world.

John 16:33 MSG

Merriam-Webster Dictionary Definition: A strong desire sometimes mixed with doubt, fear, or uneasiness.

Anxiety and fear go hand in hand. Anxiety is a reaction to fear known and unknown. When you experience any type of life changing event, such as a diagnosis of breast cancer, you have a sudden, urgent response. I remember when my surgeon told me I had breast cancer. He touched the lump and confirmed it several days later with a biopsy. My whole young 32-year-old life flashed before my eyes. Every milestone, every achievement, every goal, every family event, and every happy moment replayed repeatedly in my mind. I couldn't concentrate on anything; I was restless and had trouble sleeping. Every time I would try to fall asleep or focus on positive things, I would have thoughts of dying like my mom or being extremely ill from the cancer treatment. All I could think of was getting the tumor out of my body. The days went by slowly. I tried to do things to occupy my time. I prayed. I cleaned. I baked. I researched information about cancer on the internet. I talked about my feelings with my immediate family, extended family, and Ronnie, my boyfriend at the time. I just wanted the cancer out of me. I wanted things to be normal again!

Worry weighs us down; a cheerful word picks us up.
Proverbs 12:25 MSG

When anxiety began to cover me like a blanket, I started to pray and ask God for His love to engulf me and for Him to hold me in His arms. What I needed in those moments could not be satisfied naturally. It was a spiritual battle. I needed God to intervene into my situation and turn it around for my good. I would pray and write in my journal every day. I would only listen to music by Yolanda Adams. My favorite songs were "The Battle Is The Lord's" and "In The Midst of It All," which I played over and over again. I also attended church when I was feeling well enough to go. God can meet you right where you're at. Spend time with Him and make it a priority in your daily life. It's a relationship!

And we know [with great confidence] that God [who is deeply concerned about us] causes all things to work together [as a plan] for good for those who love God, to those who are called according to His plan and purpose.

Romans 8:28 AMP

Prayer: *Father, You said in your word you are my comfort and my strength, help me to be secure in my relationship with you. When feelings of anxiety overshadow me, remind me of your promises. Thank you for turning it all around for my good. In Jesus' name, amen.*

What feelings of anxiety are you experiencing? How can you process those emotions?

3
FEELINGS OF HOPELESSNESS

God, the one and only— I'll wait as long as he says. Everything I hope for comes from him, so why not?
Psalm 62:5 MSG

Merriam-Webster Dictionary Definition: Having no expectation of good.

I found a lump in my right breast while I was in the shower doing a monthly self-breast exam. Thoughts of my mom suffering and dying from cancer raced through my mind. I refused to accept that I had a lump, even though I felt it. Ronnie, my boyfriend at the time and soon-to-be caregiver, was in the living room. I walked up to him and asked him if he felt a lump. He calmly said yes and advised me to call my doctor right away. I called my primary care physician and made an appointment. Dr. Fusion gave me a clinical breast exam and told me that the lump felt like my rib bone, however, he felt a smaller lump in my breast. My doctor knew my family history, so he was able to make a quick decision. I was then referred for a mammogram and a sonogram. From that point on, I felt like I was in a whirlwind. I was feeling a variety of emotions: fear, denial, hopelessness, and panic, just to name a few. I remember thinking to myself, I have my whole life ahead of me and now I have been given a death sentence.

> *I've learned by now to be quite content whatever my circumstances. I'm just as happy with little as with much, with much as with little. I've found the recipe for being happy whether full or hungry, hands full or hands empty. Whatever I have, wherever I am, I can make it through anything in the One who makes me who I am.*
>
> **Philippians 4:13 MSG**

Three or four days later, Dr. Crump called again and said, "The tumor was malignant." I hung up the phone and began to cry. The feelings of hopelessness and sadness deepened. I called my family, Ronnie, and Mrs. Ethel, my manager at that time. Then, everyone began to pray. I was on vacation from work, so I did not have to worry about facing anyone. How could I respond to their questions when I didn't know the answers myself? It felt as though the bottom fell out of my perfectly planned life. I never would have thought that my plans for better would be derailed by the big C. All the hope that I had, vanished like the sun on a cloudy day. In my hopelessness, God kept track of every tear, every ache and every toss and turn through my sleepless nights. Little did I know at that time, but God had other plans for my life. He took something that happened for the bad and turned it around for the good. Through my journey, I found my purpose and started Young Survivors Network, Inc. We are a support program for young women, 40 and under, diagnosed with breast cancer. Invite Him into your journey.

> *I know what I'm doing. I have it all planned out—plans to take care of you, not abandon you, plans to give you the future you hope for.*
> ### *Jeremiah 29:11 MSG*

Prayer: *Father, you know the beginning from the end. You know the plans you have for me. I will wait with hope and expectation with my whole heart and being. I put my hope in you. In Jesus' name, amen.*

Who can you call to help you get through this tough time? What changes can you make to help you feel better?

CHARRON WALKER.

4
FEELINGS OF DEPRESSION

None of this fazes us because Jesus loves us. I'm absolutely convinced that nothing—nothing living or dead, angelic or demonic, today or tomorrow, high or low, thinkable or unthinkable—absolutely nothing can get between us and God's love because of the way that Jesus our Master has embraced us.

Romans 8:39 MSG

Merriam-Webster Dictionary Definition: A state of feeling sad; low spirits.

I went from the mountaintop to the valley, from joy to depression, and from hope for the future to no hope at all. The treatments were a difficult hurdle to overcome. Each medication I took had bad side effects. I was battling mentally, physically, and emotionally to survive. My doctor put me on the lowest dose of Paxil to help me sleep because I had insomnia, depression, and nightmares. At one point,

I was put on Ambien. This medication is a sleep aid, but I stopped taking it because it was too strong. I can remember lying on my bed and praying to God to take me home because I didn't have the strength to go on. I would rather be in Heaven with my mom than suffer through this. Each round of chemo got harder and harder because it weakened my immune system. God was there with me through those dark times, He was my light in the darkness.

The nights of crying your eyes out give way to days of laughter.
Psalm 30:5 MSG

In 2009, on the night before Thanksgiving, I was attending a church called The Praise Tabernacle. We had an opportunity to let God and others know what we were thankful for. I made God a promise that if I had the chance, I would share my testimony. The whole day I was nervous because I was sharing a part of my life that was personal to me. I thought about not going to church at all, or when it was almost my turn, to go to the restroom. Pastor Steve started on the right side of the sanctuary and asked people to come up to the front and give their testimony.

I knew when it was going to be my time to speak, so I sat and waited. Then, it was my turn to share. I was nervous and not sure if I would recall everything. I prayed and walked up to the front of the church and said, "I am thankful for a peaceful night's sleep, because I remember when I had insomnia and depression and had to be put on a low dose of Paxil. I thank God for sweet dreams because I remember when I had nightmares. I thank God for healthy teeth and gums, because I remember when I had blisters in my mouth. I thank God for healthy fingernails and toenails, because I remember when they turned purple and would fall off." There was a list of things I was thankful for and put in my toolkit for future reference. I had adopted a spirit of thankfulness even in the storm. There is always something to be thankful for, you just have to look through grateful eyes.

> *Why are you down in the dumps, dear soul? Why are you crying the blues? Fix my eyes on God—soon I'll be praising again. He puts a smile on my face. He's, my God.*
>
> **Psalm 42:11 MSG**

Prayer: *Father, I thank you for never leaving me and keeping me close to you. I thank you for your love that surrounds me and keeps me safe. You said in your word, weeping may endure for a night but joy cometh in the morning. In Jesus' name, amen.*

Since being diagnosed have you felt depressed? Have you reached out to family, friends, a support group or your physicians for assistance?

....

....

....

....

....

....

....

....

....

....

....

....

....

....

....

....

5
FEELINGS OF ANGER

Since this is the kind of life we have chosen, the life of the Spirit, let us make sure that we do not just hold it as an idea in our heads or a sentiment in our hearts, but work out its implications in every detail of our lives.

Galatians 5:25 MSG

Merriam-Webster Dictionary Definition: A strong feeling of displeasure.

Being diagnosed with breast cancer erupted a variety of feelings, one of which was anger. I was never angry at God for the new journey I was on, I was angry at the circumstances that interrupted the plans I had for my life. I had big plans, or so I thought, which vanished with one word: "*cance*r." Not understanding why can also cause anger. Why was I diagnosed with cancer? Why is this happening to me? What did I do wrong to deserve this? Why me? I remember when I was a guest on The Today Show with Joan London for breast cancer awareness month and was asked by one of the producers a thought-provoking question. Are you angry with God? I responded, "No I'm not angry at God, He was there with me through it all. He was my strength, my hope, and my comfort." When you are faced with any type of life changing experience, you have two choices. You can either turn to God or turn away from Him. I chose to turn to Him and let God overshadow me which deepened my relationship with Him. It's a very thin line between love and hate. Choose love!

> *Go ahead and be angry. You do well to be angry—but don't use your anger as fuel for revenge. And don't stay angry. Don't go to bed angry.*
> **Ephesians 4:26 MSG**

Prayer: Father, there are goals and plans that I want to achieve. I don't always have the answer to circumstances that happen in my life. You said in your word "For I know the plans I have for you," declares the LORD, "plans to prosper you and not to harm you, plans to give you hope and a future. I don't know what tomorrow holds, but I know who holds tomorrow. In Jesus' name, amen.

Are you angry about your diagnosis? What can you do to work through these feelings?

MADE WHOLE DEVOTIONAL

6
FEELING CONFUSED

Let my cry come right into your presence, God; provide me with the insight that comes only from your Word.
Psalm 119:169 MSG

Merriam-Webster Dictionary Definition: Being perplexed or disconcerted.

Confused does not begin to explain my mind set at that time. I was a young woman starting my life after finishing graduate school. I was so happy to graduate and put that part of my life behind me and move forward. I was working full time and going to school full time. It was a lot, but it was worth it! There were many sacrifices, long nights, tears, and achievements. But it was finally over, and I could breathe a sigh of relief. The sigh of relief quickly became a gasp of confusion when I was told I had cancer. I was speechless and was unable to process this terrifying news.

How could this happen to me? What is going on? Why is this happening? When did this intruder invade my body? Where do I start? Who said I could handle this?

> *When the going gets rough, take it on the chin with the rest of us, the way Jesus did. A soldier on duty doesn't get caught up in making deals at the marketplace. He concentrates on carrying out orders. An athlete who refuses to play by the rules will never get anywhere. It's the diligent farmer who gets the produce. Think it over. God will make it all plain.*
>
> **2 Timothy 2:7 MSG**

Sometimes circumstances happen in our lives that we don't understand. Honestly, we may never comprehend them. It took a long time for me to process my new way of life, because it was life changing! I don't know why I was "chosen" to walk this road, and I may never know. But I am thankful that God was and still is walking with me and has been the only constant in my life.

Even though I don't have the answers to the how, what, why, when and where, I know the One who has the explanations, and I can find comfort and peace in that.

Prayer: *Father, even when I don't know all the answers you are there with me, giving me your comfort and hope. Help me to lean on and trust in you when I am perplexed with life's challenges. In Jesus' name, amen.*

Are you feeling confused about why this happened? How can you begin the healing process?

7
FEELINGS OF PANIC

Don't fret or worry. Instead of worrying, pray. Let petitions and praises shape your worries into prayers, letting God know your concerns.

Philippians 4:6 MSG

Merriam-Webster Dictionary Definition: A sudden overpowering fright.

I found a lump in my right breast while I was in the shower doing a monthly self-breast exam. Thoughts of my mom suffering and dying from cancer raced through my mind. I refused to accept that I had a lump, even though I felt it. Ronnie, my boyfriend at the time and soon-to-be caregiver, was in the living room. I walked up to him and asked him if he felt a lump. He calmly said yes and advised me to call my doctor right away. I called my primary care physician and made an appointment. Dr. Fusion gave me a clinical breast exam and told me that the lump felt like my rib bone; however, he felt a smaller lump in my breast. My doctor knew my family history, so he was able to make a quick decision. He then referred me for a mammogram and a sonogram. From that point on, I felt like I was in a whirlwind.

> *You who sit down in the High God's presence, spend the night in Shaddai's shadow, say this: "God, you're my refuge, I trust in you and I'm safe!"*
> **Psalm 91: 1:16 MSG**

The doctor said I would lose my hair two weeks from the date of my first treatment, and he was right. It was in December, two weeks before Christmas. I was getting ready to meet Ronnie for dinner and I went to curl my hair and strands came out with the curling iron. I had a moment of panic and felt physically sick. I fought back tears and I left to go to dinner. As I sat at the table talking and eating, I remember how difficult it was for me to share this with Ronnie. Would he understand how I felt about losing my hair? What would he think about me now? Would I still be beautiful to him? Would he still love me even though my physical appearance had changed? Would he stay with me, or would he walk away? I finally expressed my thoughts, and as always, he was there to support me. A couple of days later, the day before Christmas Eve, I decided to cut my hair. I was standing in my bathroom, looking in the mirror and pulling my hair out of my scalp. I did not feel anything because the roots were dead. Ronnie wanted to stay and support me, but I told him this was something that

I had to do by myself. My hair was long, thick, and past my shoulders. Those close to me knew that I loved my hair.

We are taught, as children, that a woman's hair is her glory. It is a big part of her physical appearance. I got my scissors, and as I began to cut my hair, I cried. I felt like it was the beginning of the end for me. My identity was in my hair, and now, that beauty was lying in the bathroom sink. Would people see me as being ugly now? Would people laugh at me? Would my family and friends still accept me for who I was? Ronnie called to check on me to make sure I was okay, but he felt helpless. I did not sleep well that night. The next day when I woke up, I went to the bathroom and looked in the mirror. My head looked like a vanilla milk dud. There were patches of hair all over my head. My worst nightmare was coming to pass. I knew this day was coming, so a month before I started treatment, I had purchased a wig that was styled in the way I used to wear my hair.

I lost all my hair except for my eyebrows and eyelashes. I was scared to wash my face. I would wash around my eyes, so I would not touch my eyebrows and eyelashes. I did not want them to fall out too. I showered and put on my wig. Ronnie came over and brought my Christmas gifts with him. We were exchanging presents on Christmas Eve. We sat on the couch, and he asked me to take off my wig, I shook my head no. My self-esteem was gone. I felt so bad on the inside. I was young and I didn't have any hair. I had scars on my body, and I was depressed. I thought he would not be attracted to me anymore. I finally took off my wig to show Ronnie my head. He hugged me, then he picked up a bag that was on the floor and pulled out a pair of clippers he had bought. Then he tenderly took me by the hand and led me to the bathroom and began cutting off the rest of my hair. As he was cutting my hair, he was gentle and took his time. When he was done, he looked at me and said, "You are still beautiful." He hugged me, kissed me, and told me that he loved me. The Lord knew that I would need someone to take care of me during this most difficult time. God took care of every intricate detail of my journey. He is a good father and He is faithful.

> *Pile your troubles on GOD's shoulders—he'll carry your load, he'll help you out. He'll never let good people topple into ruin.*
>
> **Psalm 55:22 MSG**

Prayer: *Father, you are my refuge and safe place during the storms that I face. Cover me in your protection and keep me safe. When thoughts of panic and worry come, help me to lean into you. In Jesus' name, amen.*

Are you panicking about hope for the future? What steps can you take to ease these thoughts?

MADE WHOLE DEVOTIONAL

8
FEELINGS OF DENIAL

So Jesus said to the Jews who had believed him, "If you abide in my word, you are truly my disciples, and you will know the truth, and the truth will set you free.

John 8:32 MSG

Merriam-Webster Dictionary Definition: Refusal to admit the truth or reality of something.

Denial can be tricky when facing the truth head on. I was in denial after feeling the lump, I was in denial after Ronnie felt the lump, I was in denial after my mammogram and sonogram, I was in denial after Dr. Crump felt the lump and told me it was cancer. Once, the pathology report came back malignant, that was when reality and the truth firmly set in. I knew the odds were stacked against me because of my age and family history, but I still had trust in God.

> *Stand firm then, with the belt of truth buckled around your waist, with the breastplate of righteousness in place.*
>
> **Ephesians 6:14 MSG**

My appointment with the surgeon finally came. Carol, a Reach to Recovery volunteer with the American Cancer Society, sat and talked with me while I waited. When she shared with me that she was a breast cancer conqueror, I had a glimmer of hope for the future. She was well dressed, she looked healthy, and she was happy. Carol gave me information about breast cancer and the resources they had available. I was still numb and in denial. Unfortunately, when life gave me this lemon; I was not able to make lemonade. Others tried to keep my spirits up by staying positive and encouraging, but I had to accept the truth and choose whether I was going to fight or give up. I chose to fight! Keep fighting and don't give up.

> *The LORD is near to all who call on him, to all who call on him in truth.*
>
> **Psalm 145:18 MSG**

Prayer: *Father, thank you for helping me accept the truth about situations and circumstances in my life and not live in denial. I know through your strength and wisdom; I can navigate these challenges and live in freedom. In Jesus' name, amen.*

Have you taken the time to accept and process your breast cancer journey? What things can you implement to bring comfort along the way?

9
FEELING OVERWHELMED

> *Is anyone crying for help? G<small>OD</small> is listening, ready to rescue you. If your heart is broken, you'll find G<small>OD</small> right there; if you're kicked in the gut, he'll help you catch your breath.*
>
> **Psalm 34:17-18 MSG**

Merriam-Webster Dictionary Definition: Completely overcome or overpowered by thought or feeling.

On October 19, 2000, I had a lumpectomy. Seventeen lymph nodes were removed. There was no lymph node involvement, thank God; the cancer was contained in the breast. I was so grateful and relieved that the cancer had not spread to the lymph nodes. I was diagnosed with stage one infiltrating ductal carcinoma, and the tumor was 1.8 cm in size. I was frightened beyond words. I had never had a major operation before, so all of this was new to me. Fears of dying on the operation table and not waking up from the anesthesia ran through my mind. Would they be able to revive me if something went wrong? Did the cancer spread after the biopsy was done? If Dr. Crump had to make a last-minute decision to either preserve or cut off my breasts, what choice would he make?

I tried to keep my research on the internet to a minimum. I would only search on specific sites that I trusted and that had current and accurate information. There were too many opinions and too much inaccurate data. This added to me feeling as though there was no light at the end of the tunnel. The operation went well, thank God, and I was on the road to recovery. The next day I went home, and the healing began. I knew God was near, but I felt so far from Him. I was happy to have the cancer out of my body, and I was ready for the next step on my personal journey. When you are feeling the waves of being overwhelmed, be still, take a deep breath and look up. Peace be still.

> *My grace is enough; it's all you need. My strength comes into its own in your weakness.*
>
> **2 Corinthians 12:9 MSG**

Prayer: *Father, during those times when I am feeling overwhelmed help me to lean on you. When I am weak you are strong. Thank you for your grace, your mercy, and your strength. In Jesus' name, amen.*

Are you feeling overwhelmed? How can individuals in your support system help you?

MADE WHOLE DEVOTIONAL

10
FEELING STRESSED

God is a safe place to hide, ready to help when we need him.

Psalm 46:1 MSG

Merriam-Webster Dictionary Definition: Subjected to or affected by stress.

When I heard the word "Cancer" my stress level went through the roof. It was a very overwhelming time. It was a lot to accept and take in. It seemed as though my whole life flashed before my eyes in a matter of minutes. The whole process was stressful; the appointments with my primary care physician, my oncologist, my radiation oncologist, my gynecologist and my breast surgeon, the information overload, the chemo treatment and side effects, the radiation treatment and side effects, the hormone therapy for five years and the side effects, the lumpectomy and the side effects, losing friends, feeling physically and mentally sick, the uncertainty, just to name a few. But God was still in control! Despite it all He was and still is the only constant in my life. He gives the best hugs and will hold you in His arms. Let God comfort you and bring you peace.

> *Pile your troubles on GOD's shoulders—he'll carry your load, he'll help you out.*
> **Psalm 55:22 MSG**

There were some things I implemented and incorporated into my daily life that helped to minimize the stress. I was in such a low place in my life, that I had to make positive changes to my environment, and to the people I let get close to me. I would pray and write in my journal every day. I would play my favorite songs repeatedly. I attended church when I was feeling well enough to go. I burned aromatherapy candles so I could smell a sweet fragrance, and it also helped me to relax. I hugged my teddy bear, and I went for walks to be in God's presence.

The sun on my skin, the smell of the flowers, the smell of fresh-cut grass, and seeing and hearing the birds chirping, let me know that God was still there. I kept positive and supportive people around me. I was physically weak, but I was spiritually strong.

When I get really afraid, I come to you in trust.
Psalm 56:3 MSG

Prayer: *Father, You said in your word to cast all my cares upon you because You care for me. Help me to humble myself and seek You for strength. Help me to tap into your presence. In Jesus' name, amen.*

Where is your stress level on a scale from 1-10? Have you started to identify techniques that help?

CHARRON WALKER.

11
FEELING WORRIED

Don't let this rattle you. You trust God, don't you? Trust me.

John 14:1 MSG

Merriam-Webster Dictionary Definition: Mentally troubled or concerned; feeling or showing concern or anxiety about what is happening or might happen.

I had a scare in June 2007. My gynecologist found a polyp on my uterus, which is a side effect of one of the cancer medications I took, Tamoxifen. This drug may cause uterine cancer. I was worried sick and thinking the worst. I thought to myself, "Not again." I did not have the strength to go through treatment a second time; I just couldn't. I cried and I prayed, "God, You said I was healed. I can't go through this again. I need You." The polyp was benign and was successfully removed. Even though the cancer is out of my body, I still face challenges every day. I have learned that everything I go through is to help someone else. God showed up again strong on my behalf. He is faithful! My faith in God has strengthened and my relationship with Him is beyond words. He is the love of my life, and He makes the impossible possible. Trusting God should be a lifestyle!

> *Don't fret or worry. Instead of worrying, pray. Let petitions and praises shape your worries into prayers, letting God know your concerns. Before you know it, a sense of God's wholeness, everything coming together for good, will come and settle you down.*
>
> ***Philippians 4:6-7 MSG***

Prayer: *Father, when I am concerned or troubled about things I can't control or the unknown, help me to lean on You. Thank You for Your peace that surpasses all understanding. In Jesus' name, amen.*

Are you worried about the toll this will take on you and your family? Have you shared your concerns with your loved ones?

12
FEELINGS OF FRUSTRATION

In this godless world you will continue to experience difficulties. But take heart! I've conquered the world.
John 16:33 MSG

Merriam-Webster Dictionary Definition: A deep chronic sense or state of insecurity and dissatisfaction arising from unresolved problems or unfulfilled needs.

My third treatment was pushed back because my white blood cells were too low. I had to take Leukine shots every day to build my system back up. I went back to my office and sat at my desk. I was so disappointed that my treatment was postponed. I just wanted to be done with all of this. I remember talking to my family on the phone and telling them I couldn't do this anymore. They encouraged me and said that I had to do this to get better. My co-worker, Gary, walked into my office to check on me and I just broke down from frustration. He listened, gave me a hug, and said,

"It's going to be okay." I went into Mrs. Ethel's office, my manager at the time, and sat down and said to her, "I am a strong person, but this breaks you down to your lowest low." As I began to weep, she held me in her arms. We cried together and prayed. Mrs. Ethel asked for God's strength, peace, and comfort to come on me. She was also a breast cancer conqueror, another angel handpicked by God. The Lord knows what you need at the right time. He is an on-time God! He places people on assignment in the gaps of your life.

> *If your heart is broken, you'll find GOD right there; if you're kicked in the gut, he'll help you catch your breath.*
>
> ***Psalm 34:18 MSG***

Prayer: *Father, when I feel like I can't go on, I want to give up and life's disappointments are too much to bear, help me to look to You. Give me the wisdom to recognize and accept the help You bring into my life during my time of need. In Jesus' name, amen.*

Have you experienced any frustrating moments on your journey? How did you push through the frustration?

13
FEELING NEGATIVE

Keep vigilant watch over your heart; that's where life starts.

Proverbs 4:23 MSG

Merriam-Webster Dictionary Definition: Marked by features of hostility, withdrawal, or pessimism.

There are both positive and negative effects of cancer on all types of relationships: intimate, friendships, co-workers, and family. I have always kept my circle small and filled with individuals that are supportive, prayerful, and encouraging. There were times when I became negative, not with people, but with the many processes of my journey. I had made a conscious decision to surround myself with positive people who want to see me win in every aspect of my life. I look at life and my relationships differently now. Life is too short to waste on unforgiveness, confusion, and negativity. I don't worry about the small stuff, and I choose my battles. I put my trust in God, and I strive to live life to the fullest. One of the lessons that I've learned is that God is greater than anything you can encounter in your life!

> *Summing it all up, friends, I'd say you'll do best by filling your minds and meditating on things true, noble, reputable, authentic, compelling, gracious—the best, not the worst; the beautiful, not the ugly; things to praise, not things to curse.*
>
> **Philippians 4:8 MSG**

Prayer: *Father, when I begin to have thoughts of negativity, help me to change my mindset and renew my mind with thoughts of Your goodness. In Jesus' name, amen.*

Do you look at life differently now? What changes have you made to live life to the fullest?

CHARRON WALKER.

14
FEELING DOUBTFUL

The fundamental fact of existence is that this trust in God, this faith, is the firm foundation under everything that makes life worth living.

Hebrews 11:1 MSG

Merriam-Webster Dictionary Definition: Giving rise to doubt or uncertainty; open to question.

Mrs. Ethel was a breast cancer conqueror and a Christian, which was a double blessing. When she hired me to work in The Learning Center at St. Vincent's Hospital, she said, "You have a master's degree. What are you doing here?" I responded jokingly, "I need a job." After being diagnosed with breast cancer, I knew, without a shadow of a doubt, why I was there. She accompanied me to my mammogram and sonogram appointments. My family lived in New York, so God gave me an extended family in Florida. Mrs. Ethel prayed with me before I went in for my tests, then she sat outside in the waiting area. She also accompanied me when I had my appointment with the surgeon. There was so much uncertainty and doubt with the whole process: lumpectomy, chemo, radiation, and five years of hormone therapy, because all I had were memories of my mom. Every now and then I look at the pictures I have of the two of us. Since she died when I was a baby, I don't remember her, but I am told that I look just like her. When my mother went through her personal journey with breast cancer, I was very young. I did not have the opportunity to witness her struggles, fears, and concerns. I was not able to draw on her experiences. So, I had to figure out what to do all by myself. At that instant, I missed her more than ever before. God had it all planned out. He was the light in my darkness. Learn to push pass the doubt and trust the One who has it all in His hands.

The One who called you is completely dependable. If he said it, he'll do it!

I Thessalonians 5:24 MSG

Prayer: *Father, when I begin to doubt, and feelings of uncertainty begin to rise. Help me to give it all to you. Give me the strength to build my faith in you. In Jesus' name, amen.*

Are you feeling doubtful about the treatments? How can you push past the doubts?

CHARRON WALKER.

15
FEELING DISCOURAGED

> *Haven't I commanded you? Strength! Courage! Don't be timid; don't get discouraged. God, your God, is with you every step you take.*
>
> **2 Timothy 1:7 MSG**

Merriam-Webster Dictionary Definition: To deprive of courage or confidence.

I went for walks to be in God's presence. The sun on my skin, the smell of the flowers, the smell of fresh-cut grass, and seeing and hearing the birds chirping, let me know that God was still there. I kept positive and supportive people around me. I was physically weak, but I was spiritually strong. The spirit of discouragement tried to come on me so many times. I wanted to give up and throw in the towel. I was in the fight of my life. I was fighting physically, mentally, emotionally, and psychologically. The devil doesn't fight fair. He hits you when you are at your lowest. But the

Bible says in Ephesians 6:11-13, "Put on the whole armor of God, that you may be able to stand against the wiles of the devil. For we do not wrestle against flesh and blood, but against principalities, against powers, against the rulers of darkness in this age, against spiritual hosts of wickedness in the heavenly places." Questions would pop in my head: Why did this happen to me? Where is God now? Is the cancer coming back? What did I do wrong? I held on to the promise, "With His stripes I am healed." Jesus took it all on the cross. Keep that in the forefront of your mind.

He knows us far better than we know ourselves, knows our present condition, and keeps us present before God. That's why we can be so sure that every detail in our lives of love for God is worked into something good.
Romans 8:28 MSG

Prayer: Father, when I feel discouraged and want to give up. When the weight of the battle is overpowering help me to remember Your promises. In Jesus' name, amen.

Do you feel like giving up? What can you do to persevere through those tough times?

16
FEELINGS OF SADNESS

If your heart is broken, you'll find G<small>OD</small> right there; if you're kicked in the gut, he'll help you catch your breath.

Psalm 34:18 MSG

Merriam-Webster Dictionary Definition: Affected with or expressive of grief or unhappiness.

I called my family and shared with them what happened at my appointment and what the next steps were. They began to pray and be supportive. That night Ronnie came by and stayed with me as long as I needed him. We held each other more than we talked that night, because the mountain we were facing together was bigger than both of us. The days went by slowly. I tried to do things to occupy my time. I prayed. I cleaned. I baked. I researched information about cancer on the internet. I talked about my feelings with my immediate family, extended family, and Ronnie. I just wanted the cancer out of me. I wanted things to be normal again! A couple of days later, I got a call from Dr. Crump, who said he needed to run more tests and that I was not out of the woods. A flood of feelings came over me. I felt some hope that this nightmare might be over. I thought that maybe Dr. Crump had made a mistake when he said it was cancer. After all, how could he make a diagnosis just by touching the tumor? A glimmer of hope was better than no hope at all. My dad was angry that the doctor thought it was cancer just from feeling the lump without having the results from the tests. I assured my father that Dr. Crump was a specialist and that he knew what he was doing. Sadness is an emotion, if not managed, can turn into depression. The Bible says, "The joy of the Lord is our strength." In those challenging moments, learn to depend on God for His joy and peace.

Three or four days later, Dr. Crump called again and said, "The tumor was malignant." I hung up the phone and began to cry. The feelings of hopelessness and sadness deepened. I called my family, Ronnie, and Mrs. Ethel. Then, everyone began to pray. I was on vacation from work, so I did not have to worry about facing anyone. How could I respond to their questions when I didn't know the answers myself. When all your hope is gone turn to God. He will never leave you or forsake you!

Don't let this rattle you. You trust God, don't you? Trust me.

John 14:1 MSG

Prayer: *Father, when I am sad help me to look beyond the circumstances and what I see in front of me and to look to You. In Jesus' name, amen.*

How are you processing these feelings? Is there someone you can talk to?

MADE WHOLE DEVOTIONAL

17
FEELINGS OF URGENCY

Seek God while he's here to be found, pray to him while he's close at hand.

Isaiah 55:6 MSG

Merriam-Webster Dictionary Definition: The quality or state of being urgent.

Feelings of urgency swallowed me after receiving the news that my lump was malignant. In my mind I did the math; Mommy passed away at 33 from breast cancer + getting diagnosed at 32 + more aggressive cancer = dying. There was an urgency to get the cancer out of my body quick, fast and in a hurry. Just the thought of having a tumor, this thief, trying to steal my life and my future, in my body gave me an urgency to fight. I had to war against the mental and psychological battle I was having, the unanswered questions and the unrest. There was so much unknown. Was the tumor still growing? What was the staging? Was there any lymph node involvement. I was so grateful and relieved that the cancer had not spread to the lymph nodes. If it had, that would have been a totally different diagnosis, mindset and treatment plan. Even with the feelings of urgency, I still had the peace of God below the surface. That was my firm foundation and the rock on which I stood.

> *You can be sure that God will take care of everything you need, his generosity exceeding even yours in the glory that pours from Jesus.*
> **Philippians 4:19 MSG**

Prayer: Father, You know all, and You see all. You know the beginning from the end. Help me to see through spiritual eyes, that it will all work out for my good. In Jesus' name, amen.

Do you see yourself as a survivor or a conqueror? Do you feel the urgency to fight?

18
FEELINGS OF INSECURITY

You know me inside and out, you know every bone in my body; You know exactly how I was made, bit by bit, how I was sculpted from nothing into something.

Psalm 139:14 MSG

Merriam-Webster Dictionary Definition: A state or feeling of anxiety, fear, or self-doubt.

Relationships are difficult enough when there is no crisis but imagine being diagnosed with breast cancer at a young age, going through treatment, fighting for your life, trying to keep things as normal as possible, and being involved in a relationship. When treatment begins, you deal with many levels of personal inadequacies: mental, emotional, psychological, and physical. You tend to feel that you are not physically attractive anymore. Low self-esteem creeps in because you lose your hair or because of the scars on your body. Unfortunately, these feelings are real and tend to stay with you even after treatment ends. Ronnie became my caregiver. We had dated for a year before I was diagnosed with breast cancer. He moved from boyfriend to caregiver in a short period of time. God handpicked Ronnie to help me through this season. He was there every step of the way, and I never heard him complain. He was scared because all of this was new to him, and it affected someone very close to him that he loved. Ronnie shared with me, a few months after treatment began, that he looked at himself in the mirror and said, "Ronnie, you got to step up to the plate." And that he did! He took me to my chemo treatments, shaved my head, prayed with me, made sure I ate, listened when I needed to talk, and cried with me when I did not understand. He was patient, he supported me, and encouraged me when I wanted to give up. Ronnie also told me that when I would be sleeping, he would look at me and pray to God to give me strength. He could have walked away, but he didn't. I was never concerned about that, because I knew that God had chosen him to be in my life and for that I am thankful. My cancerversary is on his birthday, so I can never forget his kindness. God already knew what I needed and who I needed in my life during that time. God is truly amazing! Trust Him to know what you need and who you need in your life during your journey.

Embracing what God does for you is the best thing you can do for him. Don't become so well-adjusted to your culture that you fit into it without even thinking. Instead, fix your attention on God. You'll be changed from the inside out.

Romans 12:2 MSG

Prayer: *Father, thank you for knowing my insecurities and still loving me. Help me to see myself as You see me. Help me to trust the process. In Jesus' name, amen.*

Are you feeling insecure about yourself or your relationship? How can you communicate those feelings to your significant other?

CHARRON WALKER.

19
FEELING ANXIOUS

Don't fret or worry. Instead of worrying, pray. Let petitions and praises shape your worries into prayers, letting God know your concerns. Before you know it, a sense of God's wholeness, everything coming together for good, will come and settle you down. It's wonderful what happens when Christ displaces worry at the center of your life.

Philippians 4:6-7 MSG

Merriam-Webster Dictionary Definition: Characterized by extreme uneasiness of mind or brooding fear about some contingency.

My hair started to grow back. It was curly like a newborn baby's. I was ecstatic to see peach fuzz sprouting. This growth let me know that the chemo was out of my body and the toughest hurdle was over. I only wore my wig out in public, so when my hair started to grow back, I was self-conscious. The first time I put on my wig to go out in public,

I was going to work. I felt anxious and uncomfortable. As I looked in the mirror to brush my wig, I thought, this is really happening. There was no turning back now. I could either accept my new look or I could hide. That morning, Gary, my training partner at the time, and I were teaching a class and one of the students said, "Charron, you have such a peace around you." I began to share with her that I was receiving chemo treatment for breast cancer. I told her that I had lost my hair, and I was wearing a wig. She replied, "I would have never known." Her words brought reassurance to me. I might have looked different on the outside, but on the inside, I was still the same. *Jesus Christ is the same yesterday, today, and forever.* When you have a relationship with God your inner man is renewed day by day.

> *Give your entire attention to what God is doing right now, and don't get worked up about what may or may not happen tomorrow. God will help you deal with whatever hard things come up when the time comes.*
>
> **Matthew 6:34 MSG**

Prayer: *Father, You said in your word to be anxious for nothing; Instead to pray about everything. When those feelings arise, help me to pray and thank you for all You have done. In Jesus' name, amen.*

Do you have a comfort level with your "new normal"? How can you begin to embrace it?

20
FEELING ASHAMED

What matters is not your outer appearance—the styling of your hair, the jewelry you wear, the cut of your clothes—but your inner disposition.
I Peter 3:3-4 MSG

Merriam-Webster Dictionary Definition: Feeling inferior or unworthy.

Growing up I was always shy, and I never wanted the spotlight on me. I was never an attention seeker. When opportunities arose to shine, I ran and hid. A couple of months ago, I began to look at my life and the journey I took to get to this point. Every experience in my life has prepared me for this moment: from working with different types of people to managing a budget for an after-school program, my relationship with God, each job I held, each class I took, each challenge I encountered, my father being a bishop, each valuable lesson learned, and each individual that was in my life for a season. All these things were pieces of the bigger picture. I had no idea that one day I would be the founder of a support program for young women who were diagnosed with breast cancer. I definitely did not think I would have cancer. Because I am a private person and my self-esteem was on empty, I felt ashamed and uncomfortable when asked about my breast cancer journey. To me, that was personal. But I quickly realized that my testimony could help someone else. How can I be God's heart if I am ashamed of what I went through and fearful to share my journey. Now, if an opportunity arises, I share my testimony with everyone without shame or fear. I have learned that everything I go through is to help someone else. You are not just a survivor; you are a conqueror!

> *You're beautiful from head to toe, my dear love,*
> *beautiful beyond compare, absolutely flawless.*
>
> **Song of Solomon 4:7 MSG**

Prayer: *Father, I am thankful for the opportunities You have given me and the doors You have opened for me to share your faithfulness and goodness. I pray they see You and not me. In Jesus' name, amen.*

What encouraging words would you share with someone newly diagnosed? How would you uplift others along the way?

CHARRON WALKER.

21
TOOLS FOR YOUR TOOLKIT

Finally, my brethren, be strong in the Lord and in the power of His might. Put on the whole armor of God, that you may be able to stand against the wiles of the devil. For we do not wrestle against flesh and blood, but against principalities, against powers, against the rulers of the darkness of this age, against spiritual hosts of wickedness in the heavenly places. Therefore, take up the whole armor of God, that you may be able to withstand in the evil day, and having done all, to stand. Stand therefore, having girded your waist with truth, having put on the breastplate of righteousness, and having shod your feet with the preparation of the gospel of peace; above all, taking the shield of faith with which you will be able to quench all the fiery darts of the wicked one. And take the helmet of salvation, and the sword of the Spirit, which is the word of God; praying always with all prayer and supplication in the Spirit, being watchful to this end with all perseverance and supplication for all the saints. Ephesians 6:10-18 NKJV

FEELINGS OF FEAR

Even when the way goes through death valley, I'm not afraid when you walk at my side. Your trusty shepherd's crook makes me feel secure. Psalm 23:4 MSG

....

Don't panic. I'm with you. There's no need to fear for I'm your God. I'll give you strength. I'll help you. I'll hold you steady, keep a firm grip on you. Isaiah 41:10 MSG

....

When I get afraid, I come to you in trust. Psalm 56:3 MSG

....

Be strong. Take courage. Don't be intimidated. Don't give them a second thought because GOD, your God, is striding ahead of you. He's right there with you. He won't let you down; he won't leave you. Deuteronomy 31:6 MSG

FEELINGS OF ANXIETY

I've told you all this so that trusting me, you will be unshakable and assured, deeply at peace. In this godless world you will continue to experience difficulties. But take heart! I've conquered the world. John 16:33 MSG

....

Worry weighs us down; a cheerful word picks us up. Proverbs 12:25 MSG

....

And we know [with great confidence] that God [who is deeply concerned about us] causes all things to work together [as a plan] for good for those who love God, to those who are called according to His plan and purpose. Romans 8:28 AMP

FEELINGS OF HOPELESSNESS

God, the one and only— I'll wait as long as he says. Everything I hope for comes from him, so why not? Psalm 62:5 MSG

....

I've learned by now to be quite content whatever my circumstances. I'm just as happy with little as with much, with much as with little. I've found the recipe for being happy whether full or hungry, hands full or hands empty. Whatever I have, wherever I am, I can make it through anything in the One who makes me who I am. Philippians 4:13 MSG

....

I know what I'm doing. I have it all planned out—plans to take care of you, not abandon you, plans to give you the future you hope for. Jeremiah 29:11 MSG

FEELINGS OF DEPRESSION

None of this fazes us because Jesus loves us. I'm absolutely convinced that nothing—nothing living or dead, angelic or demonic, today or tomorrow, high or low, thinkable or unthinkable—absolutely nothing can get between us and God's love because of the way that Jesus our Master has embraced us. Romans 8:39 MSG

....

The nights of crying your eyes out give way to days of laughter. Psalm 30:5 MSG

....

Why are you down in the dumps, dear soul? Why are you crying the blues? Fix my eyes on God—soon I'll be praising again. He puts a smile on my face. He's, my God. Psalm 42:11 MSG

FEELINGS OF ANGER

Since this is the kind of life we have chosen, the life of the Spirit, let us make sure that we do not just hold it as an idea in our heads or a sentiment in our hearts, but work out its implications in every detail of our lives. Galatians 5:25 MSG

....

Go ahead and be angry. You do well to be angry—but don't use your anger as fuel for revenge. And don't stay angry. Don't go to bed angry. Ephesians 4:26 MSG

FEELING CONFUSED

Let my cry come right into your presence, God; provide me with the insight that comes only from your Word. Psalm 119:169 MSG

....

When the going gets rough, take it on the chin with the rest of us, the way Jesus did. A soldier on duty doesn't get caught up in making deals at the marketplace. He concentrates on carrying out orders. An athlete who refuses to play by the rules will never get anywhere. It's the diligent farmer who gets the produce. Think it over. God will make it all plain. 2 Timothy 2:7 MSG

FEELINGS OF PANIC

Don't fret or worry. Instead of worrying, pray. Let petitions and praises shape your worries into prayers, letting God know your concerns. Philippians 4:6 MSG

....

You who sit down in the High God's presence, spend the night in Shaddai's shadow, say this: "GOD, you're my refuge, I trust in you and I'm safe!" Psalm 91: 1:16 MSG

....

Pile your troubles on GOD's shoulders—he'll carry your load, he'll help you out. He'll never let good people topple into ruin. Psalm 55:22 MSG

FEELINGS OF DENIAL

So Jesus said to the Jews who had believed him, "If you abide in my word, you are truly my disciples, and you will know the truth, and the truth will set you free. John 8:32 MSG

....

Stand firm then, with the belt of truth buckled around your waist, with the breastplate of righteousness in place. Ephesians 6:14 MSG

....

The LORD is near to all who call on him, to all who call on him in truth. Psalm 145:18 MSG

FEELING OVERWHELMED

Is anyone crying for help? GOD is listening, ready to rescue you. If your heart is broken, you'll find GOD right there; if you're kicked in the gut, he'll help you catch your breath. Psalm 34:17-18 MSG

....

My grace is enough; it's all you need. My strength comes into its own in your weakness. 2 Corinthians 12:9 MSG

FEELING STRESSED

God is a safe place to hide, ready to help when we need him. Psalm 46:1 MSG

....

Pile your troubles on GOD's shoulders—he'll carry your load, he'll help you out. Psalm 55:22 MSG

....

When I get really afraid, I come to you in trust. Psalm 56:3 MSG

FEELING WORRIED

Don't let this rattle you. You trust God, don't you? Trust me. John 14:1 MSG

....

Don't fret or worry. Instead of worrying, pray. Let petitions and praises shape your worries into prayers, letting God know your concerns. Before you know it, a sense of God's wholeness, everything coming together for good, will come and settle you down. Philippians 4:6-7 MSG

FEELINGS OF FRUSTRATION

In this godless world you will continue to experience difficulties. But take heart! I've conquered the world. John 16:33 MSG

....

If your heart is broken, you'll find GOD right there; if you're kicked in the gut, he'll help you catch your breath. Psalm 34:18 MSG

FEELING NEGATIVE

Keep vigilant watch over your heart; that's where life starts.
Proverbs 4:23 MSG

....

Summing it all up, friends, I'd say you'll do best by filling your minds and meditating on things true, noble, reputable, authentic, compelling, gracious—the best, not the worst; the beautiful, not the ugly; things to praise, not things to curse.
Philippians 4:8 MSG

FEELING DOUBTFUL

The fundamental fact of existence is that this trust in God, this faith, is the firm foundation under everything that makes life worth living. Hebrews 11:1 MSG

....

The One who called you is completely dependable. If he said it, he'll do it! I Thessalonians 5:24 MSG

FEELING DISCOURAGED

Haven't I commanded you? Strength! Courage! Don't be timid; don't get discouraged. GOD, your God, is with you every step you take. 2 Timothy 1:7 MSG

....

Put on the whole armor of God, that you may be able to stand against the wiles of the devil. For we do not wrestle against flesh and blood, but against principalities, against powers, against the rulers of darkness in this age, against spiritual hosts of wickedness in the heavenly places. Ephesians 6:11-13

FEELINGS OF SADNESS

If your heart is broken, you'll find GOD right there; if you're kicked in the gut, he'll help you catch your breath. Psalm 34:18 MSG

....

Don't let this rattle you. You trust God, don't you? Trust me. John 14:1 MSG

FEELINGS OF URGENCY

Seek GOD while he's here to be found, pray to him while he's close at hand. Isaiah 55:6 MSG

....

You can be sure that God will take care of everything you need, his generosity exceeding even yours in the glory that pours from Jesus. Philippians 4:19 MSG

FEELINGS OF INSECURITY

You know me inside and out, you know every bone in my body; You know exactly how I was made, bit by bit, how I was sculpted from nothing into something. Psalm 139:14 MSG

....

Embracing what God does for you is the best thing you can do for him. Don't become so well-adjusted to your culture that you fit into it without even thinking. Instead, fix your attention on God. You'll be changed from the inside out. Romans 12:2 MSG

FEELING ANXIOUS

Don't fret or worry. Instead of worrying, pray. Let petitions and praises shape your worries into prayers, letting God know your concerns. Before you know it, a sense of God's wholeness, everything coming together for good, will come and settle you down. It's wonderful what happens when Christ displaces worry at the center of your life. Philippians 4:6-7 MSG

....

Give your entire attention to what God is doing right now, and don't get worked up about what may or may not happen tomorrow. God will help you deal with whatever hard things come up when the time comes. Matthew 6:34 MSG

FEELING ASHAMED

What matters is not your outer appearance—the styling of your hair, the jewelry you wear, the cut of your clothes—but your inner disposition. I Peter 3:3-4 MSG

....

You're beautiful from head to toe, my dear love, beautiful beyond compare, absolutely flawless. Song of Solomon 4:7 MSG

THE CONQUEROR

By
Thomas Mortimer

When grey skies appear due to a dreadful diagnosis
and storm clouds gather because of a gloomy prognosis,
the bright light of my Savior will shine within me,
as He destroys every weapon formed against me.

Negative people will not invade my life,
I put away all bitterness, anger and strife.
Unforgiveness will have no place in my heart,
God's Perfect Love has given me a fresh start.

If chemotherapy results in the loss of my hair,
I refuse to be downcast and I will not despair.
My Lord molded me and shaped me to be more like Him
therefore, my beauty radiates from down deep within.

When friends are scarce and loved ones begin to flee,
I know my God will never leave nor forsake me.

It's in my weakness that His Glory is revealed,
so by His stripes I proclaim that "I am healed!"

The work of the Cross says I am not defeated,
the plan He has for my life will be completed.
Through my tears of anguish from the struggle and pain,
I have faith in Jesus that I will rise again!

So as God guides the steps of my journey,
I hereby embrace my new identity:

I am a Child of the King,
in Him I can do anything.
I am Daddy's Beautiful Princess,
His Eternal Love for me is priceless.
I am a Lady of Elegance,
His Grace and Mercy flow in abundance.

I am an Unshakeable Believer.
I am a Relentless Survivor.
I am a Courageous Warrior.
I am an Invincible Overtaker.
I am a Victorious Overcomer.

I AM A BREAST CANCER CONQUEROR!

Lessons Learned

Lesson #1: It's just hair; it will grow back.

Lesson #2: Everyone makes mistakes; we're only human.

Lesson #3: Your physical appearance does not define who you are.

Lesson #4: Life is short. Live it to the fullest.

Lesson #5: Don't sweat the small stuff and choose your battles.

Lesson #6: Don't make other people's issues your issues.

Lesson #7: As long as God knows my heart, that's all that matters.

Lesson #8: My mate has to accept me for who I am. No exceptions!

Lesson #9: You don't realize how strong you are, until you have to flex those muscles.

Lesson #10: God's plan is not our plan.

Lesson #11: It isn't over until God says it's over.

Lesson #12: Learn a new word: "Whatever!"

Lesson #13: One day at a time.

Lesson #14: God is greater than anything you can encounter in your life.

Lesson #15: I never would have made it without God in my life.

Lesson #16: It's in God's strength, not mine, because when I am weak, He is strong.

Lesson #17: My scars (inside and outside) are proof of battle. I was fighting to live.

Lesson #18: People are in your life for a season.

Lesson #19: True friendship is through the thick and the thin.

Lesson #20: Trust God in spite of what it looks like.

Lesson #21: I am a conqueror

ACCEPTING WHAT LIFE BRINGS

Anything in life that we don't accept will simply make trouble for us until we make peace with it.

There are the countless situations in just one twenty-four-hour period that we can't control.

No matter how forcefully we try, we can't manage to change the many things in our life we'd like to change.

Learning to accept what we can't control becomes habitual with enough practice.

The profound relief of knowing that we're not responsible for every decision, every situation, and every person in our life will feel like the best blessing we've ever received.

Today I will accept my life and serenity of letting go.

—Author unknown

END NOTE

Information taken from *My Purpose God's Plan* by Charron Walker, © 2013 by Charron Walker. Used by permission of Charron Walker.

Information taken from *Merriam-Webster.com,* © 2024 Merriam-Webster, Incorporated.

ABOUT THE AUTHOR

Charron Walker is the CEO/Founder of Young Survivors Network, Inc., and a published author of *My Purpose God's Plan*. She is a breast cancer conqueror and an educator on breast health. Charron is an active volunteer with American Cancer Society, Reach to Recovery Program. She is a Certified Mental Health Coach. But to those who know her well, she's a kindhearted and down to earth city girl who is thankful that God chose her to be His heart and to help other young women on their breast cancer journey. Young Survivors Network, Inc. was founded in 2006. Charron lives in Florida.

Website: www.youngsurvivorsnetwork.org

Facebook page: https://www.facebook.com/YoungSurvivorsNetworkInc/

Instagram page: https://www.instagram.com/YoungSurvivorsNetworkInc/

ABOUT YOUNG SURVIVORS NETWORK OUTREACH MINISTRY, INC

We are a support program for young women, 40 and under, diagnosed with breast cancer. Our mission is to educate, support and advocate for young women who have been diagnosed with breast cancer. We also equip these women in our community with information and a network of caring members, that are willing to give them the best chance available to cope with cancer.

Our My Sister's Keeper Program is a multi-faceted initiative.

We provide temporary assistance and support for women, 40 and under, undergoing treatment for breast cancer at no cost to the participant. Services include, but are not limited, to house cleaning during chemo or radiation treatment, assistance with purchasing a wig, assistance with doctor and prescription copays. The MSK Program helps to relieve some of the day-to-day pressures of managing a family and home while undergoing chemotherapy, radiation or lymphedema treatment for primary diagnosis or metastases of breast cancer.

We have a Facebook Online Support Group for women, 18 and older, living with chemo brain from treatment.

Outreach in our communities to educate women on breast health, early detection and living a healthy lifestyle.

Young Survivors Network, Inc.

Support program for women, 40 and under, diagnosed with breast cancer.

www.youngsurvivorsnetwork.org

Follow us on Facebook and Instagram

Young Survivors Network, Inc.

www.ingramcontent.com/pod-product-compliance
Lightning Source LLC
LaVergne TN
LVHW051841080426
835512LV00018B/3007